It is the author's opinion that religion should have an acknowledged place in the academic course of study, but that it should be primarily on the "mind" level. Further, it should be offered but never imposed.

It is likely that both churchman and educator may disagree with parts of this book. But it is certain that both will profit from reading it.

Biblical Thought and the Secular University is the third volume of the Rockwell Lectures at The Rice Institute to be published by Louisiana State University Press. Earlier volumes are listed on the back of this jacket.

THE AUTHOR—

GEORGE A. BUTTRICK has accepted appointment as the 1960-61 Harry Emerson Fosdick Visiting Professor at Union Theological Seminary in New York City.

His previous books include *The Parables of Jesus, Jesus Came Preaching, The Christian Fact and Modern Doubt, Prayer, Christ and Man's Dilemma, So We Believe, So We Pray, Faith and Education*, and *Sermons Preached in a University Church.*

He is general editor of the twelve-volume series, *The Interpreter's Bible,* and of the forthcoming *Interpreter's Dictionary of the Bible.*

Dr. Buttrick has served as guest preacher in many American universities, including Yale, Princeton, Columbia, Cornell, Stanford, Dartmouth, and Duke.

GEORGE ARTHUR BUTTRICK

Biblical Thought
and the
Secular University

Louisiana State University Press

Baton Rouge

Copyright 1960 by
Louisiana State University Press
Library of Congress Catalogue Card Number: 60-13168
Manufactured in the United States of America by
Vail-Ballou Press, Inc., Binghamton, New York
Designed by Ernst A. Seemann

To all my colleagues at "Fair Harvard"
—those who agree with the plea of this
little book and those who disagree—
whose friendship, accordant or discord-
ant, has opened for me new gateways into
"Veritas."

Preface

❖

THIS LITTLE BOOK IS A RESCRIPT OF THE ROCKWELL Lectures given at Rice Institute in February, 1959. Actually only two of the three lectures were delivered: pressure of work forbade my staying more than two days in Houston, and President Houston graciously "waived" the third lecture (chapter two in this book) on the understanding that all three would be printed.

The topic chosen seems appropriate for many reasons. It falls squarely within the generous and discerning terms of the Lectureship, as the reader will quickly recognize. It is a live issue both for the college and the church. It has long been one of my own "concerns," as witness the little book published some time ago entitled "Faith and Education." Many years in the church and the recent years when I have been privileged to preach and teach in Harvard University have given a background of experience which has rekindled the concern and enriched my understanding.

One long shelf of my library is filled with books on this theme. They have been treasure, truth, and cause for gratitude. But this book is not a compendium or remarshaling of materials on that shelf, as the footnotes to these pages will show: the references are to "wider" fields. The value of a book is in its original thought. So I have "started afresh." This book is a new endeavor, even though it is greatly indebted directly and indirectly to finer minds. Perhaps this rethinking may bring some gift to a topic which is now crucial both for the college and the church.

It is a glad obligation to thank President W. V. Houston and Professor Niels C. Nielsen, Jr., of the Department of Philosophy in Rice Institute, and other members of the faculty for their singular kindness during the days of the lectures, and also the eager audience of faculty and students who made the delivery of the lectures a privilege and joy. Gratitude is offered also to many friends in Harvard, not only to those who agree with the convictions here expressed, for those who disagree have taught me much: they have clarified and corrected my own thinking. I hope these chapters may contribute to the keen-minded and friendly debate which must precede any reorientation of education within the wonderful relevance and "ultimate concern" of Biblical thought.

GEORGE A. BUTTRICK

Sequanota Club,
Charlevoix, Michigan.

Contents

❖

Biblical Thought and the *Secular University*

1
Assumptions
and Presumptions

❖

THE TERM "BIBLICAL THOUGHT" DOES NOT IMPLY any literalism or bibliolatry, but simply the thinking and the faith set forth in the Bible. "Biblical" differentiates this faith both from other schools of thought such as the ancient gnostic or the modern positivist, and also from the major religions. Biblical thinking cuts across other schools of thought, Platonic thought for example; and as for the religions, our thin resolve on "tolerance" hides the fact that, though there is beneath all faiths a common ground—universal or general revelation, the aboveground structures may have little in common. To take but one item: Oriental religions regard history as illusion or a treadmill fate, whereas Biblical faith believes that history is so real that God himself is revealed within it in a once-for-all encounter with our human life. In such a conflict where decision is required, truth is ultimate, and love is ultimate, the honoring of each man's freedom as he seeks (or is sought by) truth; but tolerance is not ultimate: it may be a condescending evasion or a self-righteous clouding of counsel. There is a further and existential reason for our choosing the term "Biblical Thought": our American culture, in which perforce we live, rests on it far more than we realize.

The term "Secular University" acknowledges that even colleges originally rooted in the Biblical tradition now tend to disown their roots or to strike secular ones. Higher education, in the necessary "divisions" of our interests and functions, is primarily concerned with the mind-aspect of man's response to total Reality—in short, with truth. It makes room for goodness, if only in courses in ethics, and for beauty, if only in the study of the fine arts; but its paramount concern, especially in recent years, has been with truth, not least but dominantly, with scientific truth. Thus the typical university tends to dismiss the Bible as a vague and sentimental affair called "religion," as an unwarranted intrusion, as "indoctrination," or at best as a matter for private conscience. We shall inquire if this dismissal has warrant. But present facts require us to use the title "Secular University." These two main terms as we now describe them are pointer-readings rather than blueprints, but if we keep Shakespeare's warning in mind—"Define, define, well-educated infant" [1]—they may serve our purpose. The ground thus cleared, we discuss certain assumptions and presumptions.

I

The church has sometimes assumed that it has final truth, with right to impose it. As a matter of fact, the university naïvely assumes that truth is a land of total information and knowledge toward which the mind presses and which it shall one day reach, and that then truth will be a final requirement. But let us limit ourselves for the moment to the dogmatism which the church has sometimes sponsored and prescribed. This dogmatism has been accompanied by a moralism. Therefore the university has rightly resisted what it calls "religious indoctrination." Whenever the church says "this creed is final," it has closed the circle. But to close any circle is to admit a realm of mystery beyond the circle, which admission at once falsifies the claim of finality. This the university dimly knows, despite its frequent assumption that truth is a land of total information achievable one day by man's finite mind. So the university is on guard against church dogmatisms, not without cause and occasion.

It is important to recognize that all creeds, whether scientific or churchly, are symbolic, if only because all language is symbolic. As for scientific creeds, though they may be true of man's life in the natural order, they are a poor index of his power to stand above the natural order. As for churchly creeds, they are manifestly symbolic: "sitteth on the right hand of God the Father Almighty" [2] cannot be literally true unless God has hands like our hands and a throne like our thrones. The admission that all creeds and language are symbolic does not invalidate them. Logic, spacial measurement, scientific analysis, and propositional statement may be the media of truth about man's life in the natural order, but they hardly touch his strange power to view himself in the natural order. There the proper language is myth, symbol, drama, and history. Thus we may claim validity for the church's creeds. But by that same token they are to be offered, not imposed.

As for the church's moralism, that has been a worse

blight. Not all Freudian doctrine need be accepted out-of-hand, but it would be hard to refute its tracing of the baleful effects of churchly moralisms.[3] Once again the resistance of the university to this kind of indoctrination has been justified, even though the university has not always clarified the reasons. Telling people what to do is coercive, conceited, and a waste of time. It is coercive because it tries to steal another man's decision and because it treats him as object rather than as subject; conceited, because it pretends to a better knowledge of the other man's mysterious and secret life than perhaps he himself dares claim; and a waste of time, because honorable folk do not obey such coercion and conceit.

All this is written in partial defense of the characteristic attitude of higher education toward the Bible and the church. A creed and, still more, a moralistic code of conduct can never cover the new situation in our ever-developing world. Besides, a creed or code grants little power to the man who would keep it and may only anger the man resolved not to keep it; and it has perhaps too little to say to the man who has self-accusingly broken it, though in that regard a creed is far better than a code. The church's "thou shalt" must always be suspect and brought to test, and its "thou shalt not" still more suspect. An old lady whom I knew and honored, whose sayings were worthy of print, delivered herself one day as follows: "I'm against the Ten Commandments because they put ideas into your head." The saying needs scrutiny, but it meanwhile blows away some rubbish. So higher education should resist indoctrination but might remember that, if there is no "live option" to secularism, secularism itself may become a dogmatism.

II

So we turn now to certain assumptions of secular education which may themselves have become unwittingly a blind or coercive creed. What of the cult of "objectivity"? Behind the college mind there is sometimes a glib formula: secularism equals objectivity; objectivity equals truth. None of these three terms is "pure," each is ambiguous or "mixed," and the equations themselves when they are examined bring no conviction. Secularism —the word comes presumably from *saecula*: of the age— is itself an assumption, namely, that man is only of time and space. But who can know? The secularist may be very surprised one minute after death. Similarly the term objectivity begs the question, for it is not possible to separate the thing seen from the seeing eye. The world in which we live is not "a realm of natural law," for that description is so fragmentary as to be almost false, but rather a world in which natural law and human freedom are indissolubly joined. Likewise with the word truth: we may not safely assume that it is a time-space land of total information which some day will be organized into complete knowledge, for truth may be God's self-revelation, and it must answer man's total nature, not merely his empirical mind. Since each term in the double equation is ambiguous and perhaps an abyss, what becomes of the equation itself? It is at best naïve, and at worst a refusal to confront life's dimension of depth.

Secular education, rife with assumptions false or true, borrows some of them from Biblical faith. The college thus rests on the "indoctrination" which it is quick to condemn. Science assumes that the universe is a *universe*: one song; but this is an assumption, the more so when we remember that the universe is "open" and that the exploration of it may hardly have begun. This taken-for-granted unity is almost certainly derived from the Biblical faith that "the Lord our God is one Lord" [4] and from the epistemological depth in which we know, in the unity of our own personhood, the confrontation of the one Reality. Science further assumes that matter is worth studying, but perhaps only Biblical faith has thus regarded matter. Other faiths have deemed man's body and the cosmos an illusion or a prison or a fetter on the "soul," but the Bible declares that "the earth is the Lord's." [5] It follows therefore in Biblical thought that man is a psychosomatic unity, a paradox of person in whom the body is not less precious (because essential) than the psyche. Science further assumes that time is a straight line of purposeful change, so that a hypothesis may safely be followed by experiment, and that in its turn by tentative conclusion. But this view of time is strictly Biblical, for outside the Bible men have assumed that time is cyclic and that life is a squirrel cage. The fact that science rests on Biblical faith is not solely a "church" claim: men not in the church, such as Alfred North Whitehead,[6] have acknowledged it.

Perhaps a point has now been reached in our argument at which it can properly be said that all our knowledge is built on faith. Men who constantly plead "objectivity" live in a house that would have no foundation if men of faith had not "dug deep" [7] into the rock. There is, there can be, no strictly objective history, for every historian deals with only a handful of the facts and then marshalls this small group around a faith in "what is important." That is to say, every historian chooses his stance and can hardly ignore the Man who split history into before and after. It is no disparagement of the writing of history, but rather a tribute, to say that the histographer's art is a form of dramatic literature feeding both on the facts and on the mind. If higher education is to continue as a quest for or an apprehension of truth, requirement now rests on the college and university to examine and reappraise its hidden assumptions.

III

Let us consider an assumption shared by both the household of faith and the world of higher education, namely, *a belief in progress.* We have become almost slave to certain words. One of them is the word "values," a sorry word with a price-tag always somewhere in the offing, a plural word which, if taken literally, would make us polygamists in faith. Another such word is "progress." It has become an idol which, like all idols, finally destroys its worshipers. Thus the church has spoken about "The Ascent of Man." [8] If man is finite, creaturely, dependent, contingent—surely we cannot pretend otherwise!—how can he hope of himself to "ascend"? Perhaps he can be lifted, but he can hardly climb. The doctrine of man's "ascent" led to a liberalism in theology which events of the last fifty years have trag-

ically refuted, to a church stained deeply with a bourgeois ideology, and to the Marxist heresy of an inevitable
dialectic in history and a revolutionary power in man
that together (so the claim runs) must usher in the perfect world.

The educational variant of the belief in progress is
seen in such phrases as "the evolution of learning" or in
the euphoria perpetrated at a recent educational conference: "The mind of man: horizon unlimited!" The
term evolution has some claim on man's life in the natural order, though even there room must presumably be
left for locked types and reversions to type; but if man
has any stance above the natural order, an ability to view
that order and his own life in it, he has power to flout
and destroy his "evolution." Dachau [9] is hardly proof
of "the ascent of man" or of an "evolving intelligence,"
still less of "progressive" sainthood. Modern man views
time (without any profoundly pondered doctrine of
time!) as a sequence of evolving generations and deduces
thus that recorded history is but a few minutes of man's
"years" on earth. Then he becomes intoxicated with his
own words, exclaiming, "Give the race another million
years!" Leaving aside the permissible prognosis that
under atomic threat the race may not have another million hours, it is plain that the last fifty years have be-
queathed a mixed legacy: good and evil. Why should
not the same fact hold of a million years? Granted it
need not be so, that history need not be a recurrent dog-
fight; it must also be granted that man in his strange
freedom still chooses his own power-struggles rather
than some higher wisdom.

Both church and college now confront the fact that

"progress" is not necessarily such, and each must re-order life in face of that fact. Nuclear fission is not necessarily progress: it may spell the end of history. Our gadgets, which we so glibly equate with progress, are each a "could be": an automobile could be an ambulance, or it could be a gangster getaway car. Human history constantly develops, with its growing technological complexity posing an ever more crucial choice, but it does not automatically "ascend." History is not an escalator: if it were, man would cease to be man, for he would have no freedom. History is not a dry-cleaning establishment with a rotary-flow "that washes out all the dirt and lint." Time itself may be infected. It is certainly infected with transience so that "the mind of man" weakens and dies. Perhaps the phrase "the progress of the race" is itself monstrous—the death of each yearning, questing, praying man to provide manure for an abstract harvest which never arrives. Suppose we must disavow our belief in man's own progress. The issues would be momentous for both education and the church. It might require a new curriculum; already it has brought a revolution in theology.

IV

These false assumptions derive from a false doctrine of the nature of man. That issue is now a "hot spot." Theology has been obliged, under the tragedy of our times, to reopen the question of the nature of man, as has also philosophy, if only because existentialism has challenged the very term man in its bare and abstract "essence," to insist that there is only this man and that man in his *act-ual* "existence." Science must newly confront the issue or, by making man a thing, an "it," science may itself sink into the death of thinghood. Then what of higher education? Can the college conduct its ventures with any hope of fruitfulness unless it is realistic about the human nature which it would educate and in which it lives? So this chapter moves now to a brief comment about man's nature and destiny. As to the truth of the comment, the reader may judge, for he has his own human nature as testing rod.

(a)

A man lives a two-dimensional life—the dimension of time-and-space in the natural order, and the dimension from which he views himself on this timebound earth. The Biblical phrase which describes his life in history is that man is "of the dust of the ground," [10] the phrase which describes his higher stance is made in the likeness and image of God.[11] The scientist shies away from the term "supernatural" and can hardly be blamed if we remember the grotesque and arbitrary ways in which the church has sometimes used the term; but whenever the scientist says "the natural order," he has taken ground above that order and is himself supernatural. A Harvard report on higher education argued that we can judge our world only from our own culture.[12] The claim has some warrant, for no man can escape his culture, but it has no full warrant, for every man who had a hand in writing the report was capable of judging his culture, not infallibly, but with enough truth to say, "Thou ailest here and here."

We can never escape our earthbound nature: we would have more hope of escaping from Alcatraz; but we are never unaware of another level of life. As "dust of the ground" we have bonds with the animal creation: we sleep, eat, sicken, and die. As those who can view human destiny, we see ourselves on pilgrimage through "the seven ages of man." [13] To admit that we cannot escape our creaturely condition is not to condemn matter and time as evil: that dark proposal comes from gnostic (perhaps from earlier Orphic?) [14] thought. Biblical thought has no truck with the notion that *soma* is *sema* (that flesh is prison), for by Biblical thought the body and time are both by God's ordaining. Indeed, by Biblical thought, both body and psyche are candidates for "resurrection," that is to say, for rebirth in a new and shining dimension. Man, being "open to himself" [15] (Martin Heidegger's phrase), always transcends in thought his earthly existence, but he cannot of himself lift himself above the limitations of history. Is this contention true or untrue of our mortal life?

If it is true as Biblical thought holds, does it not have implications for any true education? The limits of these three chapters and my own too short experience in higher education permit here only hint of these implications. Certainly one of them is the right of Biblical thought to an important and perhaps central place in the curriculum. Students should know the Biblical faith which, like a wise home, nourished the scientific learning of our western world. Many a discipline of a modern college might thus find a surer basis for its studies.

Why any learning? The question has scant answer if life is a brief phosphorescence on an unresting sea of matter, unless we say, as probably we must, that human beings wish to know and understand as natively as they wish to breathe. But knowledge has a deeper sanction in Biblical faith. There it is believed that man is given right to "name all things," [16] the Hebrew verb meaning not merely to give a name to, but to scrutinize all things so as to learn their secret and to enter into their power. Thus science is ordained in Biblical thought, man being God's trustee. There we learn that each human being is uniquely precious; hence medicine and psychiatry receive their deeper validation. A further implication of man's two dimensional life is this: he is subject, not merely object; therefore science can give no complete account of man's mysterious life, nor can any man of any race rightly be treated as less than subject-man; and therefore democracy has its warrant: it cannot endure as a political form unless it is first accepted as a vital faith. The reader can add to these momentous implications, as in this final instance: If man is free because he can view his timebound life, and if freedom is kept only as it is practised, if man is thus a choosing and deciding creature, what becomes of the endlessly suspended judgment which marks the academic mind? Martin Buber has written that "a devil . . . would not be one who decided against God, but one who, in eternity, came to no decision." [17]

. (b)

Man, because of his two-dimensional nature, is prone to anxiety-guilt. The secular university bridles at the word guilt, and has some cause, for it has become Mrs.

Grundy's [18] moralistic stock-in-trade. Moreover, our time has learned under Freudian truth of the wide incidence of psychotic guilt. But guilt, by Biblical understanding, is neither moralistic nor psychotic, but linked endemically with the anxiety of the creature. Man's pilgrimage is on a narrow path between two orders: the natural order from which he cannot lift himself and in which he must die, and the higher order from which he views his precarious journey. Thus he chokes (the root meaning of our word anxiety). He is in "a strait betwixt two" [19] and is always tempted to play his own God. By Biblical thought, sin is the denial of our creaturehood.

This transgression takes two main forms. A man may transgress—cross one boundary of his human nature—by trying to build a heaven in the natural order, by means petty or grandiose, by cash or lust, or by the enjoyment of culture or mighty empire; or he may cross the other boundary to pretend that he is not a creature of time and space: he may pose as pure mind, as self-appointed mentor of his neighbors, or try to live in some stratospheric idealism, or propose that science of itself can build a "brave new world." [20] Baalism and titanism are the two forms of transgression, and manifestly they make havoc in our world. Man posing as an animal becomes a more cruel animal, for no self-respecting wolf would have planned Dachau; man posing as an angel or as Atlas is a feckless and muddle-headed sham, tragi-comic at last in his inflated pride. Is anxiety-guilt as long as history? Is it as wide as our world, and (in this sense only) a "total depravity"? Is the disfiguring mark set on all man's works so that each new discovery may be perverted to a "proud" use and every corporate structure twisted to human self-centeredness? The Bible does not shrink from these questions. It speaks boldly of "the grandeur and misery of man." [21]

In the ebb and flow of human history some eras seem to have been more anxious than others. The time of the breakup of the Greek city-states may have been an instance. If so, we may gather some comfort from the fact that the great age of Socrates, Plato and Aristotle sprang from that chaotic era. Almost certainly the time of the Reformation was scored by unwonted anxiety: men took to the monastery to save their souls and the souls of their neighbors in the impending end of history; and once again new and creative forces, though not unmixed with "guilt," were set in motion. Do we live in one of the anxious centuries? So it would appear. At any rate an Orson Welles radio-drama [22] about the arrival of men from Mars sent thousands into the streets in the fear that the Martians had actually arrived. Atomic threat has not caused our anxiety: it has only occasioned it by driving a shaft into that reservoir of anxiety which is hidden in every man's life. Atomic threat has made the anxiety overt instead of covert. So man becomes more frantic in the attempt to make his own security, and thus becomes his own double threat.

If this account of human nature is true, it holds consequences for both church and university. The church, at least by Protestant awareness, can "transgress": it can seek refuge in the natural order by encouraging atavistic emotions, and it can be guilty of pride by posing as a moralistic mentor or as a sinless class. By the same token the university can be guilty: in baalism it may identify man with the natural order and examine him as if he were only a more complicated insect; and in titanism or angelism it may pretend that the mind is "pure" and somehow apart from man's existential nature. Is the mind pure? Is it a little sun shining in an infinite sky? Is it not mortal and prone to error? Can it not become prostitute to evil cause? To these issues we shall turn in the second chapter.

Meanwhile, the Biblical faith that raises them is neither "indoctrination" nor sentimentalism. Practical problems also are raised. If our age is an age of anxiety, the church should not increase anxiety by playing on it or by offering a superficial healing, and the university may not ignore the foreboding of its members. Some of us are troubled by the undue numbers of students who are emotionally unstable, and we must ask ourselves if there is full justification for an educational system that practises almost forcible feeding of the brain under examination pressures. We do not know the answers and have great sympathy for college administrators who must work in an age of flux and upheaval; but we know the questions and know that they must be met, even though only fractional answers can presently be given. The questions are raised by Biblical realism; perhaps the answers can be found only in Biblical faith.

(c)

One further tenet of Biblical thought about human nature presents itself: *a man is a responsible being.* That is, he is able to respond and is called to exercise the ability. This call reflects again his two-dimensional na-

ture. He is in the creaturely order, his life contingent
and derived, but the light of another order shines down
on him in gentleness or storm. There is no escalator-
progress and no final code in either politics or morals,
but there is an unconditional demand: that a man must
print on the creaturely order "the pattern in the
mount." [23] If agricultural science provides a metal
plough to cut deeper into the soil of India and seed
better suited to Indian soil, and shows by the sinking of
clean wells that there is means of irrigation, it has become in measure sacramental, a sacrament being "the
outward and visible sign of an inward and spiritual
grace." [24] Art is of this nature; it lives by an ultimate
sanction. So are new forms of government that meet the
ever-developing relativities of history.

This Biblical interpretation of responsibility, that a
man shall obey God and "till the ground," [25] delivers
us not only from false notions of progress, but from the
bane of the problem-answer approach to life and education. In a sense life may be viewed as a problem: it
comes with existential demand, and no ideology—capitalism, communism, or churchianity—can be applied
in toto. But in another sense the "problem" approach
is a too-ready transfer from the laboratory which deals
with objects and, therefore, easily forgets that people
are also subjects. Scientism, not the rigorous humility
of true science, has encouraged the naïve idea that in this
ambiguous world and in man's amphibian nature we
can somehow find a neat formula "to solve our problems." Communism is that kind of cruel oversimplifica-
tion. So is capitalism in some of its American advocates.
So is fundamentalism in its pretense that all we need is

"to apply the clear commandments of Scripture." Even Albert Einstein could not understand why world government cannot *pronto* be adopted.

In any event, we are responsible. The neutralism of the academic mind admits as much in its phrase, "we must seek the truth." A more accurate phrase would be "must print creatively on the natural order a truth which ever and again breaks in on us." Responsibility means more than applied art and applied science, though there is no escape from that involvement. It challenges the cult of neutralism and "strict objectivity." A professor cannot be dogmatic or coercive. Biblical faith itself is not of that kind. But can he be neutral? If he should try, he has not avoided "indoctrination," for he is indoctrinating students in neutrality, in the impossible notion that they can view life without being involved in it. There is an encompassing Mystery, never resolved but often revealed, with its unconditional demand; and there is in man a response-ability. We are advocating no "do-good" ambition from the professor's desk; Jesus once asked, "Why do you call me good?" [26] But academic neutralism in Germany, then one of the best-educated nations in Europe, made a vacuum, and since human nature abhors a vacuum, the situation invited Hitler's obscene banners. The Bible doctrine of the nature of man has other tenets, notably and centrally a faith in man's redemption, and these shall shortly engage us. But these three tenets suffice our present purposes.

V

The application of this Biblical truth, if it seems truth to us, if it echoes the realities of our daily life, is a task for the educator. This writer has come too recently into academic life to presume more than the most tentative suggestion. Perhaps secularism may now be seen, in the flux of our times, as too arid a field for the questing mind. Perhaps we should say, rather, that the relativities of the secular order themselves imply the constraint of an ultimate concern. Education must now, perhaps, forswear the ideology which has led to our tragic time and strike camp, but it must still deny the moralisms and dogmatisms of which the church has sometimes been guilty, and still hold the journey to an adventure and response of mind. We can sympathize with the educator as he confronts this new demand in a new age and admire the thrusts which he has latterly made. "The Crisis in the University" [27] has become forerunner to a host of books, written in sober mind and not in sectarian zeal, on that same theme. This little book is exploratory. It can offer only a provisional guidance, for it is still largely stranger to the world of higher education.

With some assurance it is proposed that the Biblical view of man and his world should have an acknowledged place in the curriculum. If gnostic thought is taught, with its dualism of "pure" archetype and "broken" cosmos, of a mind that is "clear" while the body is the work of a dark demiurge, why should not place be found for the counterview that both *psyche* and *soma* are a Divine tion. Our apocalyptic time has not been sired by the church (though the church has doubtless been involved in its guilt and helped to provoke its heresies), for the church has latterly been despised. Our age is the child, rather, of "self-expression" and the pride of man. Biblical faith has of late either been forgotten or ruled out of court as "indoctrination." If then groups of people say, "We propose a Biblical frame for education because we believe the mind is enfranchised in that faith, not bound as in the limits of the secular view," they are not necessarily either obscurantists or dogmatists. Nor should the "bad" word "compulsory" be saddled on the church-related college. The required listening to Bach in a course in musical appreciation is not compulsory music, and epithets are not argument. If the dean of a church-related college says to an applicant, "We believe our frame of reference is a wider freedom for the mind, and that the only safeguard against idolatry is the worship of God," and if he then invites the applicant to choose, the relationship thus established is hardly "compulsory," and the college is not exhibit A of benightedness. Nor is there fear that the secular point of view will not be represented in such a college, for most history ignores Jesus, and some science thinks that nature is a self-explanatory system. Perhaps the church-related college is a needed witness in our "mixed" society. Its danger is that it may leave no place for honest doubt, which is always a cutting edge for finer faith. Yet, it should be remembered, the Bible itself includes such doubt: Job is the Albert Camus of the Bible, and Ecclesiastes is a stoic skepticism. The church-related college may yet lead our dreary factualisms from their wilderness. Surely mind should object to the method long followed in British universities: courses in Biblical thought, taught with honorable scholarship, for those who wish to take them.

Then what of the plethora of churches and creeds? When that question is asked, the secular mind often takes an angel-stance: it looks with contempt on "these religious bickerings." It is easy to avoid debate: all a man need do is to repress the ultimate questions which must always arouse crucial conflict. The problem of creeds is real and hard, but it does not justify the secular angelism, for there is no life without struggle. The secularist does not deplore controversy in other realms of learning. Copernicus did not speak peace to the then-accepted world of astrology. John Maynard Keynes, with his "The End of Laissez-Faire," [29] is hardly a soporific in the present study of economics in America. Communism has obliged honest minds, whether in theology, social theory or politics, to read and debate "The Communist Manifesto." [30] Werner Heisenberg [31] and Niels Bohr [32] have not been doves of peace to physics: they have brought consternation to the scientist who was sure that nature is a neat deterministic order. The charge that "religion brings conflict" to the campus, if widely accepted, would condemn the whole curriculum. Besides, I have noted in my limited experience that it is often the secular mind, with its strange assumption that education must be conducted in a secular framework, which starts the "religious controversy." This being said, admission must be made that the clash of creeds has often been a scandal. Yet it must be allowed also that our time has seen a more irenic mind. A good Protestant seminary, for instance, requires its students to study other faiths. There are overt rapprochements in our time, and covert mutual understandings. As example of the latter, Protestantism begins to understand the importance of church "tradition," while Roman Catholicism intensifies its study of Biblical sources: here the parts are now reversed. Meanwhile, each college and university stands in its own tradition, its own geographical area, and its own culture. Therefore it can offer first those courses, such as courses in Biblical thought, which are nearest to its own climate and life, and then add courses as student interest, professorial competence, and the needs of the time may suggest. This it could do without fearing or evading controversy, any more than it avoids the issue between the old school and the new in the field of art.

What of a university church? Newness in a secular college or university may in some localities almost forbid any such church. In other cases the college church has centuries of tradition which the college can no more disown than a tree can disown its roots or a man his memory. For such a college to try to discard its history might invite amnesia. Centers of higher education in our times seem rootless. "Learning" cannot unify them despite our common assumption: "learning" is a verb without a noun and becomes an abstraction if it has no convincing ontology of human nature. Nevertheless, it is still true that a traditional university church will always be partly anomalous and certainly ambiguous in our "mixed" society. Those of us whose job is in such churches are as acutely aware of the anomaly as are our critics. We are aware also that such a church should not ask special privilege. It should not pretend to speak for its total group. It should seek only a voluntary loyalty. It should offer its word only for those who wish to hear and should sedulously avoid "pressures." Its witness should be in a quiet lowliness.

But within such a context it may rightfully raise its crucial questions, such as this: If we do not worship God in His ultimate mystery, how can we escape the idolatries that have desolated our time? Men who do not worship God do not then cease to worship: they are caught in some form of narcissism. If a man hears in church, "The truth of the Lord endureth forever," [33] he may be less inclined to absolutize some philosophical or scientific system. If he confesses in church, "Thy kingdom is an everlasting kingdom," [34] he will not let the cheap demagogue go unchallenged. If he reads the words of Jesus, "Learn of me," [35] he may be reminded that there is a wisdom which our "learning" cannot bestow. If he comes on the words, "Lord, thou hast been our dwelling place in all generations," [36] he may glimpse what it is that binds a college to its honored past and may then find a home—even in the world of higher education.

VI

This chapter has outrightly challenged certain assumptions of church and college, in particular the naïve proposal that secularism is verity. Secularism is not objective truth, we have argued, but a faith; and we have further pleaded that our apocalyptic time is demonstrating that it is a false faith. In the next chapter we shall approach our general theme not from the gambit of Biblical thought but from an examination of the dimensions of mind. Meanwhile we offer a summation. Our colleges are in America, America is on a little swinging ball called Earth, Earth is in a corner of the solar system, the solar system is in the cosmos, and the cosmos is in an abyss of mystery; and—there is a depth in the mind of man from which he views this whole vast interplay of life and time. What of that depth? If man is the creature who can judge his own life,[37] he has one leg in eternity, even though the other leg may be in time. My friends in Harvard who disavow "religion" still do not live for the secular, the *saecula,* the age: they live for the ages against tyranny and all contempt for our humankind. Their deeds show a better faith than their lips are ready to profess. That is why the allegedly secular university brings gifts which sometimes the church fails to bring, and for which the household of faith should give thanks.

2
Reason and Revelation

❖

D ESCARTES' FAMOUS "I THINK, THEREFORE I AM" [1] HAS made trouble enough both for philosophy and theology. At risk of stirring up more dust and heat we offer
three comments: (1) The formula plainly steals the issue: the "therefore I am" is not a true sequent, for "I
think" has already insinuated the personal pronoun.
The rabbit is discovered in the hat because it has already
been surreptitiously placed there, as is inevitable in this
instance: a man by nature assumes his self-identity. (2)
The "I think" is an abstraction, for a man cannot think
without thinking about something. The formula should
run: "I think about my world, therefore I am and the
world is." Thus man's stance above the world might
have become clear. (3) The word "think" is not a single,
unmixed term, for the mind is a complexity and perhaps
an unplumbed depth. It holds conversations within itself: "Shall I pay this monthly bill or try to skip it? Shall
I yield to this sexual impulse or follow a higher value?"
Thus the word "think," though it may seem simple, is
both involved and profound. Perhaps it is an abyss and
a mystery. This third comment directs our present
journey. We ask now about the anatomy of mind. Then
we shall ask if our findings are reflected in Biblical
faith and what meaning they may have for the secular
university.

I

The theologian is frequently invited by the skeptic to "prove God to me." The invitation really means "prove it to my scientific and analytic mind" and thus is unaware of the mind's complexity. A proposition in logic may be "proved," though even in that instance axioms must first be assumed, but God is not a proposition in logic. A verdict in science may be demonstrated, for example that two parts of hydrogen and one part of oxygen constitute water, though even in that instance water is a new thing in its own right; but God is not an object or a finite entity to be demonstrated, and if He were He could not be God. Thus the demand, "prove God," may be an unwitting idolatry; for if God could thus be proved to the mind so that the mind held God in encompassing comprehension, the mind itself would be God, and God would be degraded to a theorem or an object. Perhaps the word "learning" *is* always in danger of becoming an idolatry. So we try to indicate some "levels" of the mind, not in hope of tracing any full-orbed phenomenology (that would be utterly beyond my poor competence, and indeed is not in any man's power), but of showing the complexity and depth of the formula, "I think."

There is the logical and scientific level of mind. In Biblical appraisal this mind is not "secular," but ordained. Men are given right in the Bible's judgment to "name" [2] all things. The "name" of a god means his nature as disclosed in his acts. To "name" a thing is thus to discover its secret and to appropriate its power. This understanding, which is almost a description of our science, is confirmed in the Biblical avowal that God has given man "dominion" [3] over the natural order. Of course this right to "name" and to "have dominion over" is a trusteeship, not an outright ownership nor an absolute claim. To absolutize it would be an attempt to deify the creature—a grotesque idolatry. But the trusteeship is ordained. Our science rests (unaware of its ground of support) on the Biblical convictions that the cosmos is one, that matter is precious because God made it, and that man is intended of God to understand the natural order and to have dominion over it. The trusteeship has proved both a fascination and a boon. It has also been perverted into an attempted ownership. There is no quarrel between the Genesis stories and modern science, for Bible writers always accept the science of the time in which they write: the Genesis stories are *mythos* to describe each man's present life. They trace man's finitude and God's overruling providence. The Tower of Babel [4] story, for instance, shows what happens when science is not content with trusteeship but tries to usurp ownership. Thus Biblical thought exalts, but never deifies, the logical, analytical, and scientific mind which in our time has almost been equated with the whole of mind.

But there is also the receptive and contemplative mind. The scientific mind analyzes; the receptive mind synthesizes. The scientific mind seeks to control; the receptive mind waits to be controlled. The scientific mind dissects a flower, while Tennyson in contemplative mind yearns to know it "all in all," [5] believing that thus he would know both "God and man." The two levels of mind are a complement: the analytic mind ventures, the contemplative mind builds a home. Wordsworth was once upbraided by an activist friend for "dreaming time away," though actually the poet waited in stillness for whatever word the wholeness of the world and the mystery of life might give him. So Wordsworth penned a rejoinder, which he titled "Expostulation and Reply."

> "Think you amid this mighty sum
> Of things forever speaking,
> That nothing of itself shall come,
> And we must still be seeking?" [6]

The prophets of our race stride from silence to proclaim the message of the solitude. But the receptive mind is not less a mind. A man is not less intelligent when listening to the music of Bach than when examining a precipitate in a test tube. Amos strode upon our world from desert solitudes, and Jesus came from a waiting-in-prayer to split history into before and after and to proclaim the kingdom of God.

There is the universalizing mind. It governs the philosopher's quest to unify and understand man's total life and world. It has its dangers: perhaps every level of mind is the Joseph [7] who sees himself the favored child and thus attempts to rule his brothers. Modern existentialism has uncovered another danger: the philosophic mind easily forgets its base in the actualities of a man's life; it can get lost in abstractions. Did not Sören Kierkegaard say of Hegel [8] that when he asked the philosopher in effect for directions to a street address in Copenhagen he was given only a map of Europe? Yet the universalizing mind has value, and grants an ampler wisdom.

We live actually in an instant "now" which leaves behind it a yesterday frozen into objectivity and which greets and partially creates an always-arriving tomorrow, but the concept of "time"—both *chronos* time of the wheeling planets and the *kairos* [9] time of determinative junctures in human history—enables us to think more clearly and more comprehensively about the "now" of our life on earth. Similarly the abstraction "man" is much better than an abstraction: it delivers us from captivity in our private fortunes and sets us free to think in enfranchised mind of all men—and of God "before whose face the generations rise and pass away." [10] The philosopher's "essence," as in such terms as "beauty" and "truth," and the existentialist's tang of instant self-concern may soon be seen not as an "either-or" but as a "both-and," or as an inevitable dialogue. Jean-Paul Sartre [11] may insist that a man knows only the immediacies of his own experience, but he still writes books about it which assume that other men can know something of Sartre's own life and thought. The universalizing mind leads on to what we shall soon call the self-transcendent mind.

There is the mutual mind. It is the nature of mind to flow into mind. Sometimes we assume that a man's body makes him a person, but the body in that issue is ambiguous: it gives him individuality which aids personhood but links him with the whole natural order so as to threaten personhood. Then we assume, especially in university circles, that "reason" makes a man a person; but reason also is ambiguous, for while it girds personhood by granting man power to think about his world, it threatens personhood by its proneness to flow into an-

even in our most positivist moments. A psychiatrist friend once gave me a fine simile: the conscious mind is like the pricked-out points of light of New York City seen from an aeroplane at night; the subconscious mind is the multitudinous life of New York City proceeding unseen beneath the points of light. Perhaps that description is overdrawn in favor of the subconscious. If so, it still serves to underscore a truth. Our skepticisms, for example, are not usually the fruit of brilliant questionings from honest minds. They are more likely to come as late harvest from our young rebellion against moralistic parents or against a stuffy pietistic church.

There is what Kierkegaard might call "the mind of dread." [13] In the night-watch we are aware of the mystery of the human pilgrimage. Again we attempt no self-consistent phenomenology of mind: perhaps "the mind of dread" is within the movement of what we shall call the self-transcendent mind, but it is important enough in its own right to justify this separate mention. Our race, and each man in it, has no visible port of departure, no visible port of arrival, and the journey is over an illimitable and unfathomed sea beneath an illimitable and unfathomed sky. We look at the tree just beyond the window, and we say, "It need not be there." We look at ourselves in the mirror and make the same judgment: "You need not be there." Then we run back to the apparent safety of visible things and assure ourselves, "It is nothing"; at which moment Jean-Paul Sartre taps us on the shoulder and replies, "Precisely: we live in nothingness." [14] The mind aware of "nothingness" is not less intelligent than the mind which calculates the speed of light. Archibald MacLeish has a poem describing what happened when a sudden storm blew away the "big top" of a circus:

> "there overhead, there . . .
> Those thousands of white faces, those dazed eyes,
> There in the starless dark the poise, the hover,
> There with vast wings across the cancelled skies,
> There in the sudden blackness the black pall
> Of nothing, nothing, nothing—nothing at all." [15]

There is the self-transcendent mind, of which the "mind of dread" may be but one looming component. Though we are locked within the natural order with its inevitable finitudes, we see ourselves taking that strange journey in that strange limitation. We ask ourselves, "Why should I have been born with this body, of such and such parentage, in this land, in this era of history?" The scandal of all science is the scientist, for he always defies the hope of finality in scientific tests. Whenever we say, "Mind is but the child of brain, and the injection of alcohol into the brain can determine the fashion of the thought," there is that upper man looking down on the experiment, always free from its control. The self-transcendent mind is surely the most striking fact about mind. It is the confrontation of eternity which makes us persons. It is the stance by which a scientist becomes a scientist. It is the seat of judgment from which we can appraise the culture in which we live and shape it even while it shapes us. It is the fulcrum of freedom, for it grants us liberty to view and measurably control the factors—psychological, sociological, physical, and historical—which otherwise would determine us. It is the norm by which men and policies are estimated—

the hidden "best" which justifies our verdicts of "better" and "worse." It clarifies the Biblical assurance that man is made in the likeness and image of God.[16] It is a doorway in our human life that can be opened on the infinite Mystery. It might not be too hard to "prove God" to this mind, for this mind gives warrant to the Biblical faith that "in him we live and move and have our being." [17] The blind spot of our generation concerning mind is its inability or unwillingness to see the paradoxical and ambiguous character of human reason. The mind itself is amphibian. It can navigate, though under a "mind of dread," along the shore waters of an infinite sea; it can walk, as indeed it must if it would live, on the solid ground of the natural order. But its home is not on the narrow isthmus: always it yearns for tidings from across the sea.

II

Certain comments may be in order regarding these levels of mind. The first: our present emphasis on the scientific and analytical mind has warrant, but no exclusive claim. Science has its splendid place; its rigor enables us to understand the natural order in which perforce our finite life must be lived. Our common phrase is accurate: it is "down to earth" and saves us from what might rightly be called the curse of ideology. For my own part, I never "sit in" on a theological discussion without wishing that two or three logical positivists were present to hold the conversation "down to earth." The whole mind might float in a helpless stratosphere without this firm and exact demand. But if the mind of science is the only mind, man himself must dwindle into an object, into what the existentialists rightly call the "unauthenticity" [18] of thinghood. If the scientific mind is the only mind, the experiments in the gas ovens of Buchenwald were justified. The present popular proposal that we breed a race of scientific technicians to "keep ahead of Russia" would, if followed, spell a crippling deformity of mind which in a little while would doom any scientific or technical skill.

The second comment is a question: Which is the profound and creative "level" of mind? The provisional answer is that the mind should be honored in its wholeness. The Freudian description of mind, to cite an instance, is all too thin for acceptance: there is more in mind than the *id,* the *ego,* and the *super-ego,*[19] as Freud defines them, and far, far more in personality. His formula has granted us clearer insight, but it is only a new opening gambit, not the checkmate of final understanding. Freud does no justice to the complexity and depth of mind. As more than provisional answer to the question in this paragraph, what of the Freudian mind that "looked down" to say "there is an Oedipus complex"? An upper stance, a self-transcendent dimension, in Freud's mind as in all of us, enabled him thus to judge life. That higher mind encompassed and made relatively small his Greek-mythology similes and his allegedly "scientific" formulae. Perhaps the mind cannot be understood nor rightfully employed except in emphasis upon its self-transcendence.

A third comment: the "levels" of mind as we have roughly described them almost parallel the curriculum of a modern university. The analytical and scientific mind is honored in our sciences. The logical level finds a home in logic, in our study of semantics and hermeneutics, and in mathematics, though that last-named discipline has a strangely wider range. The receptive mind seeks fulfillment through the fine arts and through the whole gamut of the humanities. The universalizing mind discovers itself and much other wisdom through the philosophies. The mutual mind takes its ventures in the social sciences, which therefore can never be strictly scientific—in economics, anthropology, and sociology. The subconscious mind is the stock in trade of psychology and psychiatry. Then what of the mind of dread and the self-transcendent mind? Levels of mind are not levels, for they are interfused. But all are under surveillance of the self-transcendent mind, and that mind is the "stuff" of faith and religion. Should it not therefore find a central place in the curriculum? Until that emphasis is recovered, our "learning" (a verb without its noun!) may be only "Hamlet" without the Prince of Denmark.[20]

III

Crucial questions must now be raised about the nature of mind, and this in particular: Is the mind pure? Greek thought proposed that simple account, and many a college professor in our time takes it for granted. To characteristic Greek thought, human reason is an emanation of the Divine *logos*. Mind is thus sharply distinguished from body and cosmos, for these are the work of a dark demiurge, a realm of imperfection, a fetter on the reason. This view of mind widely persists in our time and not alone in university circles, for many people have a vague notion that sex is unclean while reason is emancipated, or that farming is of a lower order than the practice of law. Greek thought held that man could rise by contemplation and the life of reason above the sharp intrusion of the flesh, even though complete deliverance could come only on death, when a man would be free of "this mortal coil" [21] and be reabsorbed into the Eternal mind. This view of mind was not completely and consistently held, for Greek sculpture, which is the shaping of matter, almost breathes; but it was characteristically held. Biblical thought takes almost outright issue with the Greek view of mind: "Thy sons, O Zion, against thy sons, O Greece!" [22]

Then what of the Biblical view of mind? It holds that mind is *ambiguous* because it is entangled with man's total nature and that thus it is both mortal and beyond mortality, both finite and infinite, both blundering and aware of its blunders, both pure and impure. John Dewey's proposal [23] that a clear intelligence presides over a roster of choices and that thus we find our creative way is "a thing incredible" to Biblical conviction, which would ask *instanter*: "What makes you imagine that reason is wholly pure, or wholly above man's life, or that the roster of choices (hidden in the subconscious!) is so plainly marshalled?" As for the *mortality* of the mind, it can hardly be denied: the mind sickens when the body sickens and dies when the body dies. As for the *finiteness* of the mind, can it escape limitation except in its self-transcendent term, and is it ever free from mistake? In all "the changes and chances of this mortal life" [24] human reason can make no sure predictions. Its "calculated risks" are often miscalculated; and its best intentions, however fortified by reason, often miscarry, as in the recent discovery that oxygen given to newborn babes in their extremity has an unfortunate delayed aftermath. The mind "forgets" under the sway of the subconscious, stumbles under tiredness, and blunders under sudden onset of crisis. These assertions are not assertions; they are but a transcript of every man's daily experience.

Biblical thought makes a further avowal about human reason: it can and does sin in the sense in which we have already described sin. It can sink into the natural order, selling out to cash or lust. As for the cash, big business can find scientists and artists to serve its sometimes greedy purposes; and as for pruriency, magazines that cater to lust are not devoid of brain. Hitler's "Blood and Soil" [25] enlisted both college professors and theologians. Or the mind can sin the other way—by pride, by playing its own God in intellectual titanism, by pretending that it is utterly pure, or by proposing that man can overtake all knowledge and build the perfect world. This sin of the mind is described in the Bible as "the proud imaginations of their hearts!" [26] There is a further fact regarding our allegedly "pure reason": it can rationalize. Sigmund Freud has documented that fact: the mind itself can "make the worse appear the better reason." [27] That is the death knell of any doctrine of unadulterated intellect. Yet the mind knows its own mortality, its own blundering finitude, and its own guilt. Thus Biblical faith holds that the mind, not separate

from man's total nature, is ambiguous, and that therefore the mind also is candidate for redemption.

IV

Thus we come to the whole issue of revelation. Questions which beckon that word are clear to see and easy
to state. If the mind is finite, its finitude can be overcome only by wisdom from beyond itself. If the mind is
sinful in a sense far deeper than moralistic, it can be
saved from corruption only by a purity from beyond
itself. If the mind is mortal, then its learning is mortal
and the blight of mortality is on all its works, unless it
is held in life that is sovereign over death. The concur-
rent question, "Is there such a redemption?", is not
dispassionate, though philosophy grapples with it on its
own level, namely, that of the mind's understanding: it
is every man's "ultimate concern," and the vitality of the
educational process depends on a creative answer. Revelation is not a strange intrusion, not some alien meteor
falling on our familiar fields, for our own minds are
already in touch with an eternal dimension. It is a visita-
tion, a disclosure, from within and beyond our own
minds by which we know that all our mortal learning is
held in grace and is therefore not in vain.

Paul Tillich has attempted a rationale,[28] almost an
anatomy, of revelation. Its basis and being, he says, is
Mystery: it is in a sense our own word, for it comes from
the heights and depths of our own self-transcendent
mind. Yet it is not ours because it is not by our devising
or manipulation or control; it is the self-disclosure of a

mystery which is yet never resolved. A second factor is *miracle,* by which is meant not any rending of the natural order, but an event through which the light of the Mystery streams in on us. Revelation is not through man's concepts or through any "general law," but through a happening: the "name of God" is the nature of God revealed in His mighty acts. The third item is always concomitant: *ecstasy.* This word is interpreted by Tillich not merely nor mainly in its accustomed meaning—a surcharge of lofty emotion—but in its original Greek sense: *ec-stasis,* to stand beyond. Revelation obliges us to stand beyond our life in reappraisal, because revelation is at once a judgment and a proffered grace.

As for the Mystery, the mind is constantly aware of it —or Him. For always the mind comes on antinomies, such as that of human freedom and an overruling purpose, which the mind itself can never resolve. If the Heisenberg principle is valid, there is an indeterminism even in the play of the quanta; and, as for the contingencies of our human freedom, no one can predict man's action either in the single instance or in the endless interweavings of our social life. Yet history, going its own course so that its outcome is never wholly man's intention, is so orderly, while still being vital, that it is open both to scientific analysis and to the exercise of the free mind. Meanwhile we cannot read tomorrow, much less the tomorrow of death. We live in Mystery but are aware of moments when Mystery, neither resolved nor resolvable within our finite wisdom, is nevertheless disclosed. Hitler perishing in his flame-girt cellar is judgment, not alone on him and his doctrine of "Blood and

Soil," [29] but on our whole civilization. This we instantly know. Afterwards the whole affair can be neatly ordered within psychological and sociological categories, but these are only wisdom after the event. In the eternal "now" the Mystery is disclosed; we have seen "the hid battlements of Eternity." [30]

As for the miracle-event, it can be any event, for no man knows where he may come upon his "burning bush." [31] It can be a crimson hillside in the fall:

> "Lord, I do fear
> Thou'st made the world too beautiful this year.
> My soul is all but out of me,—let fall
> No burning leaf; prithee, let no bird call." [32]

It can be an Assyrian invasion of Israel [33] interpreted as judgment on Israel's failure to keep the covenant, just as communism, no more righteous in itself than the Assyrian empire, may yet be judgment on the selfishness of a bourgeois culture. The event can be Israel's whole history. It can be the cry of a woman in an Archibald MacLeish radio play,[34] as she watched the electric letters on the Times Building telling of falling banks and failing business in the great "Depression": "*For*give us this day our daily bread!" It can be the life of a saint, as when a peasant said yearningly to St. Francis, "Good master, apply yourself to be as good as folk say you are!" [35] Who knows when the disclosing event may befall us? This question is answered in the Bible: "Our God is in the heavens: he hath done whatsoever he pleased." [36]

As for the ecstasy, any revelation lays on us a responsibility, an ability and engagement to respond. This fact holds of a new discovery in science, for such a discovery is always more than discovery: it is a gift both in the cosmos and in the strange sudden awareness (the instant of discovery) in the scientist's mind. Thereupon and thereafter the scientist is required to adjust all his thinking to the new event. This standing-outside-ourselves is just as inescapable in a "life situation." When the small plane in which two doctors [37] travel to fulfill their calling in the New Hampshire hills is forced down in winter's darkness and storm, when the search for them fails, and when months later their dying message is found: when men thus learn that the doctors spent their last days and moments making medical record of their own dying, that other men in similar extremity might profit—we are all in *ec-stasis*. To say "this is simply a matter of the body's dying, a record of a branch of science called medicine" would be almost blasphemy. It would certainly be an impossible self-evasion, for already revelation has been too quick for our rationalizing: already we have asked ourselves, "How now shall I live?"

Christian faith finds in Jesus Christ the central and controlling revelation, the *kairos* [38] or revelatory juncture in history which illuminates, judges, and fulfills all such prior *kairoi* or junctures and which is seminal for all junctures after His time. There is *Mystery* in Jesus, tidings of a world deep-within yet far-beyond: a sheer impact, which is its own evidence of both judgment and mercy. His life, death, resurrection, and continued presence are thus the sovereign *event* of our human story, with revelation in the personal term focussing and fulfilling the whole revelation of covenant history. He is the world's *ec-stasis*. He requires us, in challenge and redemption, to reappraise both our culture and our personal life. Christian faith holds that there is in Christ more than fulfillment of a rationale of revelation: He lived in obedience to the Eternal world, in a willingness to surrender all of life in the natural order and in the pride of man for that obedience, to grant us thus redemption both from "sin" and from our mortal limitations. Such a faith is not dull and small! It asks in joy of gratitude, "Does He not win every man's deepest mind? Does He not give coherence to a man's history and to the history of our race? Does He not enlighten even the enigma of pain, not by an argument, but by a revelatory Cross?"

V

What bearing do these judgments have on higher education? They do *not* require the university to become a church, though they may show the need for a church in the university. Our finite life, because it *is* finite, must be "divided" into different endeavors even though all endeavors gather in one life and one ultimate concern. A college is a venture of mind and should not be asked to forsake its own endeavor. But higher education may justifiably be confronted by the fact of the mind's ambiguity, so that it may ask in deeper intent than Pilate, "What is truth?" If the mind's ventures always fall short, always stumble, and are always stained by selfish ideologies, truth cannot be a land of "total knowledge" toward which the mind presses in sure hope

of arrival. Truth is rather that which breaks in upon
our finitude. Such is the New Testament meaning of
the word: *a-letheia*: [39] without a veil. Truth is the unveiling of a Mystery. This understanding would give a
new direction to education. The curriculum could not
then be a cafeteria of information nor a voracious search
for facts, but would become the sharing of a granted
wisdom.

An added question now claims to be answered:
Should not higher education cultivate the whole of
mind? The neglected area is that of the self-transcendent
mind, which is always unwittingly taken for granted
but rarely explored. It is the scientist's stance. Is it not
therefore more important than any isolated science? Or,
rather, should we not study the scientist in conjunction
with his science? This self-transcendence is the ground
of freedom. Is it not therefore more important than
what we call "determining" factors—historical, psychological, sociological, physical? They are "determining"
only because we have neglected the self-transcendent
term. That term is the "area" of Mystery from which
light streams and healing comes. Should it not therefore
be the crucial area of curriculum? Often it is, though
not explicitly: we study the "great" scientists, the
"great" works of literature, "great" music. By "great"
we assuredly do not mean great in the measure of human ambition, but great in granted light. We mean
what we sometimes, even in our empiricisms, call "in-
spiration"—that which is "breathed into"; we mean
profound enthusiasm—that which is *en theos,* in the god
or God! Our instinct is right:

"When the high heart we magnify,
   And the sure vision celebrate,
And worship greatness passing by,
   Ourselves are great." [40]

Yet our present studies in this area are sporadic rather than deliberate, discursive rather than penetrating and planned. The fact, the manner, the media, and the impact of revelation all call for study, as well as the "times" and the disciplines of the welcoming mind.

Beyond doubt revelation calls for a responding faith, but that necessity need not dismay us. We have shown, or tried to show, that all education rests on acts of faith. Scientific inquiry has certain accepted axioms, drawn, so we have argued, from a Biblical heritage. The writing of history depends on a "faith principle": "This is central and important." Even positivism depends on an act of faith, "The only real truth is empirical," for that avowal could never be empirically proved. The words "beyond doubt" are themselves a clue, for we doubt only what we first believe; doubt is both the road to faith and faith's astringent cleansing. Faith is the movement of our finite mind towards its infinite ground, and the movement itself is drawn by infinite beckonings. Such a faith may be the optic nerve without which we are blind to any learning and any truth. We need not defend it in higher education nor in any other endeavor: it may be at last our only defense.

3
Mutual Gifts

❖

THE CITY DWELLER IS OFTEN UNAWARE THAT HIS LIFE depends on distant fields, on the produce of the farm and the reservoir in the hills; he easily assumes that he and his neighbors live on one another by their wits. Conversely the villager often forgets the largesse that comes to him from the city, from the "city slicker" who provides farm implements from city factories and such boons as weather reports and grain-market prices by radio and television. Similarly the household of faith and the secular university may not know that they live by mutual gifts. The modern college is tempted to ask in confident voice, "What has that church on the corner to give me except a dubious architecture and a more dubious indoctrination?"; and the church may be equally prone to ask of the college, "How can that godless place enrich my life?" Both are mistaken: there are mutual gifts.

I

Let us remind ourselves of our initial working descriptions: the secular university with its graduate schools explores the universe of knowledge. The college is the *collegium,* a group of colleagues older and younger intent on the mind's adventure. The goal is

Veritas, as that single word on the Harvard shield implies; the rest of the original Harvard motto, *Pro Christo et Ecclesia,* is now usually omitted on Harvard stationery as an outgrown appendix.[1] Harvard forgets that the appendix defined the *Veritas* (*a-letheia* in the original Greek, the unveiling of Reality through Christ and the Church) and that such a definition may stand when our present thin definition of truth—an achievable land of complete information and knowledge—has gone its way into its own thin limbo. But at present truth is the concern of the university—truth as fact-finding in all its implications. Of course the curriculum includes ethic and many a practical discipline (affairs of will and conduct), together with the whole range of aesthetics (affairs of feeling), but the main intent is the mind's adventure symbolized by a student carrying books and a professor distributing the ominous examination questions.

Biblical thought we have taken to mean simply the faith set forth in the Bible. We chose that term rather than the vague term religion, because religion in our western world is dominantly Biblical and because Biblical faith stands in sharp contrast to "the world religions." It could be argued that Biblical faith is the death of "religion," for by "religion" we usually mean man's attempt to reach God, by mystic withdrawal, by some ethical and physical regimen, or by obedience to some "law"; whereas Biblical faith centrally affirms that God is God and man is man and that, therefore, the finite creature cannot reach God or even know much about Him unless God chooses to reveal Himself. Thus "religion" is an impossible upward movement from man to God, while Biblical faith tells of a downward movement from God to man—"The Word became flesh and dwelt among us." [2] Yet the origin of the word "religion" may have deep meaning for any faith or culture, including the Biblical. Perhaps it comes from *religare,* that which binds; or from *religere,* that which repeats, the verdicts to which men return and return; or from *religio,* the constraint which no man can evade. We do not know, but all three proposals are consonant with Biblical faith.

In regard to our two working definitions it is worth noting that education is a narrower land than faith, if only because the mind's adventure is not the whole of our human concern. "Learning" cannot be man's total devotion without becoming idolatrous; or perhaps we should say that learning itself is the stuff of wonder, and that wonder is the stuff of any true religion. If learning as an end in itself is self-worship, faith without gifts of mind is a land of darkness. Or to state the matter differently, though without scientific accuracy: education without faith is homeless (like the small boy at the World's Fair, with its dramatized knowledge and wonderful contrivances, who yet was found weeping—because he was lost); while faith without education is a city in which the lighting system has been short-circuited.

II

What gifts has higher education bestowed on Biblical thought? We find as we seek answer that the gifts are a vast treasure. This gift for instance: the college demonstrates a fellowship (fine name for an awarded "scholarship"!) in which prejudice of rank and race has been measurably overcome. In this regard both church and college have a spotty record. The church has taken color from a bourgeois culture, but in little more than a century has girdled the planet with farms, schools and hospitals; while colleges, historically open to men from every clime, in certain limited localities refuse to "integrate." By and large the university, together with the theater, has led the way. The impulse may have come originally from some form of religion—from the Stoic conviction that there is a Divine spark in every man, from the universalism of the Hebrew prophets, or from the Christian faith that every man is precious in the sight of God; but, whatever the origin, higher education has again and again overleapt the fences of prejudice and thus has strengthened those who would keep the edicts of Biblical faith.

Another gift has been education's defense of a rightful freedom. Again the record has been spotty; the university in Hitler's Germany lifted no banners against him, while the church made a clear protest. There are colleges even in America which do not realize that loyalty oaths can be a threat—that there is a chasm between a man's being reckoned innocent until he is proved guilty, and his being reckoned guilty unless he declares himself innocent. It should be added in digression that loyalty oaths provide cover for the communist, while they may rob the college of men of sensitive conscience. But again, by and large, higher education has defended academic freedom, even to the measure of martyrdom, and thus has been a bulwark for all true freedom. Once more it may be true that the origin of this academic resolve is hidden in religion—in the faith that marked the death of Socrates or in the central New Testament conviction that each man is uniquely a subject and that, therefore, his distinctive word must be spoken and honored. But, whatever the origin of education's *credo* of freedom, its witness has been heart of hope to all men. The Scopes Trial [3] and the attendant debate about evolution provide the instance. The college mind in that debate was resolved on fact and truth, while some churches opposed the truth and others became timid camp-followers of the college mind. If only William Jennings Bryan had understood his own real cause! He tried to defend the Bible by an impossible literalism. He should have said that the Bible itself tells us that man's life is in the natural order, and that natural science is ordained to help us understand God's way in natural creation. Then his real cause could have been lifted like a banner. It was crucial then, as it is crucial now: that man is also above the natural order, able to view his own life, and that therefore no science of itself, evolutionary or of some other kind, can either explain or fulfill man's life.

Again the realm of higher education has resisted indoctrination, and this resistance has been gift, however reluctantly received, to the household of faith. The creeds historically have been weapons of defense and should not be made weapons of attack. The defense against gnosticism, to cite only one instance, proved to be the validation of science, medicine, and economics against a view that would have condemned both flesh and cosmos. But to use creeds as attack is proselyting and a denial of a rightful human freedom. Proselyting, as psychiatry has taught us, is a mark of insecurity—the attempt of a man to drag his neighbor into his point of view, to bolster his felt inadequacy and consequent pride. Evangelizing is of another kind: the very word means the sharing of a gladness. Higher education by its resistance to indoctrination has reminded the church of its essential message. Coercive faith, still more coercive "love," is a contradiction in terms. The church's doctrine of creation, atonement, and resurrection underscores the preciousness of each human life; man is a subject, not merely an object, and therefore his freedom is to be honored. We live in an age of indoctrination, by advertising, by propaganda on a hundred different fronts, even to brain-washing. The university has sometimes been guilty of indoctrination into secularism, but it has brought gifts when it has resisted the church's lapses into proselyting and moralism.

There have been more direct gifts by higher education to the household of faith. "Higher criticism," the inquiry into the date, authorship, structure and purpose of the books of the Bible, is an unfortunate term; as is "lower criticism," the scrutiny of the word and text of the Bible; but both branches of study, however they may have raised problems in the understanding of Scripture, have been also an Open Sesame. The road to the Bible has been made more arduous, but treasures in the Bible once hidden have been brought to light. This method of Bible study was a gift from studies already in use for the classics, more particularly for the Homeric poems. Such methods are never enough for the full interpretation of Scripture, but they are necessary as an

initial and controlling honesty, and they help to reveal
the Bible's unique clarity and power. What of the gifts
of archeology? They are legion: they bring to life the
Bible word. And the gifts of historical research? There
also the church is debtor to secular learning. And the
gift of linguistics? Once more higher education has been
benefactor with a lavish hand. And the gift of psychiatry? The writer can testify gratefully, as to lectures
which he himself tries to give in homiletics and pastoral
theology, that such concepts as that of the subconscious,
of "rationalizing" and the crisscross of human motives,
of psychotic guilt and a false perfectionism, of the hurt
that comes from moralism and possessive love, have
been asset beyond price. These new understandings do
not refute the Bible: they illuminate it, giving it instance and illustration. Even chemistry now befriends
Biblical faith: it helps to determine the age of Bible
manuscripts, sometimes to the point of a minor miracle.
How many disciplines have served to elucidate the Dead
Sea Scrolls! The list is almost as long as the schools and
departments of the university!

Perhaps the best gain for faith at the hands of secular
education has been the university's insistence on truth
and fact. The church has sometimes forgotten one word
in the Great Commandment: "Thou shalt love the Lord
thy God with all thy . . . *mind.*" [4] It is easier to worship God with a brief fire of feeling or with the tear
glands. In my boyhood I was fortunate in Sunday-
school teachers, so fortunate indeed that gibes about
"Sunday-school religion" seem empty; but there was one
exception, a man who kept saying, "Do not reckon me

a thinker: I am a believer!" We took him at his word, in a way he did not intend. Unfortunately we drew the further conclusion that all faith is stupidity, a sad conclusion indeed for youngsters coming into adolescence, filled with the questionings of that tumultuous time. Truth in the study of the natural order has different tests from truth about man's life above the natural order. But college insistence that truth is self-harmonious applies to all truth. With regard to the Genesis stories, God does not say one thing on the rocks and in the Darwinian study of evolution, while saying another and a contradictory thing in Scripture. If contradiction appears, we must reinterpret either science or the Bible; or, as is more likely, both of them. The rigor of logical positivism, though it is all too small to cover man's pilgrimage, lays on every man the requirement of stringent honesty. It is a great gift that higher education should keep saying: "Face the facts. Be honest. Do not beg the question. And make the doors of a church high enough so that a worshiper need not leave his head on the sidewalk."

III

What are the gifts of Biblical faith to the secular university? Many a college professor would reckon that question absurd, if indeed it ever occurred to him to ask it. But this may be the answer: "The college professor unwittingly lives by Biblical faith. In many an instance he lives it, maybe in ways that put some churchmen to shame. He could not live *without* it in the mind's adventure." Such is the answer which this little book proposes. We now try to give chapter and verse.

(a)

One gift, in return for higher education's many bestowals, is the gift of faith itself. The Biblical view of nature is largely taken for granted by education, and the word "taken" is accurate: it is *taken* from its Biblical source. The faith that the cosmos is one and worthy of study is Biblical faith, against the view that would make matter a fetter, and flesh the evil work of some demiurge. Thus all science rests on Biblical faith. The faith that time is not a treadmill fate, but a straight line of purposeful change (not of man's purposes only), is Biblical faith; and the histographer lives and labors within it. The faith that things are not merely things but hieroglyphs is Biblical: the whole world is both instrumental and revelatory; and in that faith art, such as architecture, lives its life, stricken by radiance yet serving man's daily needs. The faith that the body is precious, an inescapable term in personhood, twin of the psyche, not a burden nor the prison of some imaginary "soul," is Biblical faith; and therein medicine finds both warrant and ordination. Western culture in its myriad boons lives by legacy of a faith which now it tries to disown. The destructive heresies of our time are heresies against Biblical thought. So the church, or God's purpose through the church, has already given to higher education the ground-of-faith on which it lives and moves—and which it often forgets. This fact holds despite the other tragic fact that the church also forgets its heritage, as when it neglects the poor to become chaplain to a bourgeois comfort.

Likewise education can receive from the Bible a faith concerning man, far more realistic than the naïve faith by which education has tried to live. Not man as "pure reason": his reason is not pure. Not man as master-intelligence: his intelligence is always short, for he is finite, and that is why his electrical skills and his air-conditioning gadgets have suddenly caused a power shortage and a black-out in New York City.[5] Not man as incipient angel: he can turn any structure, technical or political or commercial, to good or to demonic purpose. Not man with his steps on the highroad called evolution: he is relatively free and, therefore, can and does wreck any evolution unless some Grace constantly renews his onward journey. Not man who by his science is sure to fashion a "brave new world":[6] by science he can destroy the world, and presently seems intent to do it. Not man as centrally and characteristically a reasonable creature who needs only that his mind shall be educated to build a reasonable world: his reason can "rationalize" in perverted devotion to some low cause; and his center in any event is not in his reason, but in a strange awareness of his life on earth, that is, in a point of vantage above history. Not man regarded in any naïve faith, but man as potentially divine and potentially unworthy, who stands always in need of help from beyond the confines of the natural order. If education confronts this faith (it is from a Biblical heritage), education will know that the mind's adventure also, like all things human, stands in need of redemption; and it can then proceed with lowliness, and thus with the power and light which are the reward of the lowly.

But the paramount gift of faith is a realistic faith in God. The Creative Mystery, Whom men in agelong faith have called God, is not the death of meaning, but its only home. A dead certainty is just that: dead. Knowledge that is cut and dried is just that: cut and dried. There is no "complete objectivity," and if there were it would be only

> "That frost of fact by which our wisdom gives
> Correctly stated death to all that lives." [7]

A man cannot look at anything without being himself the observer. He cannot look at a fellow human as a mere object without turning him into a thing. That neighbor also is subject, because he also has a foothold in eternity. The only true knowledge of a neighbor is therefore in a subject-relationship, that is to say, in an eternal concern. The Biblical phrase is: "In Him we live, and move, and have our being." [8] Surely this Mystery, in which the mind already stands, provides vistas for the mind's adventure, more exciting and truer to the facts than the foreclosure of agnosticism or the confines of secularism. The mystery of mind refuses limits but still cannot indulge any euphoric "horizon unlimited." [9] The mind also is part of man's lot in the natural order and is therefore redeemable only by resource from beyond history. Agnosticism and secularism, like logical positivism, are faiths: they are not "objectivity." These pages plead that they do little justice either to the ever-returning verdicts of Biblical faith or to any pondered ontology of man. Thus the gift of faith.

(b)

The household of faith brings to higher education also the gift of hope. Let us try to itemize this gift. It is hope for the fulfillment of the mind's adventure. The learning process is "endless" in several ways. For one thing, it must begin again with each new generation. For another thing, knowledge is now so specialized that the various "branches of knowledge" are in danger of falling from the tree for lack of vital life: there is no common root. For still another thing, new knowledge requires new adjustments in the whole field of knowledge, and every mystery solved arouses six new mysteries from sleep. Moreover, the mind lives within constitutional limits: its wisdom is short, its predictions always partly falsified, and its future always partly unknown. The mind also must "walk by faith, not by sight." [10] My own area of study is for evidence. Once it was believed that Matthew wrote his gospel in Jerusalem about 70 A.D. That theory is not definitely shelved, but it now seems likelier that the book came from Syria towards the close of the first century. But if so, who was Matthew, and how much is the writing tinctured by the life of the early church? The new knowledge gives new understanding, but it brings also new problems. The scholar's name is Sisyphus.[11] When he is not rolling his stone, he cultivates an uncooperative farm; for though it would not be true to say,

> "Still we persist, plough the light sand, and sow
> Seed after seed where none can ever grow," [12]

it is a fact that the scholar's work is never done. Higher education rarely confronts this impasse. But Biblical thought long ago learned a fundamental honesty about all human limitations and found hope in another dimension—in God, so that the mind's adventure can say: "Now I know in part; but then shall I know even as I am known." [13]

The hope is a better hope: hope of redemption for education's failure. Admission of this failure does not justify the church, for the church also has failed. But as for education's failure, is there lack of evidence? Hitler came to a well-educated nation, and education was no bulwark against his demagogic violence. In our own land, where higher education is much more widely shared, with far more money and finer equipment, demagogues appear in a steady succession, and years pass before their meretricious plea is punctured. Radio and television are disfigured by a blatant huckstering. "Things are in the saddle, and ride mankind." [14] What price education? Judged by its results it is a costly boon. How can the failure be atoned, or rather, how is it being atoned? How has community been kept at all? It should long ago have perished in the poison of our lies—political and educational and ecclesiastical lies, white lies and black lies and grey lies. How has it survived? Not because man craves to tell the truth, for the truth eludes him, and he betrays truth. Biblical faith has an answer in which a scholar may live in grateful hope: God Himself is sacrificial love Who in His Self-offering in Jesus is "the Lamb slain from the foundation of the world." [15]

This hope has a further category: it is hope in the

confrontation of death. The word death here covers not
only every scholar's death, but the presumptive death of
all life on the planet Earth. The possibility of whole-
sale atomic death would seem to doom humanism; our
choice now is between vital faith or some form of
stoicism. If death is the final word, we may pretend that
learning has relevance, but the blight of death will rest
even on that pretense. Most scholars forget death. But
unfortunately people die, so that again and again any
man trying to evade the issue must ask himself if our
whole culture is any better than the last sumptuous
meal before the electric chair. Corliss Lamont [16] has
lately proposed a funeral service for use by humanists.
He would have the organist play Bach's "Come, sweet
death." But by what right, when Bach wrote in Christian faith? Along with Scripture he would have a eulogy
beginning, "We are gathered to do honor to. . . ." But
honor also perishes. Then he would have the leader explain: "Life and death are different and necessary aspects
of the same evolutionary process." But there is no life,
and all creativeness is doomed. Then he would quote
George Santayana's "The length of things is vanity; only
their height is joy." But the word "height" is self-decep-
tion, for the only height now is a hole in the ground. This
funeral service is an attempt, not far short of childish,
to keep faith while renouncing it. Sartre's "nothingness"
is more honest.[17] Our frequent question, "Can we live
without hope of eternal life?" may be pointless; for probably we all live by an inarticulate hope, since we all have
power to view our life in time. Biblical thought makes
articulate that hidden hope; it saves education from
corroding sadness and sets free the mind's adventure.

(c)

The other gift of Biblical thought to education is love. The whole gift is a trinity: faith, hope, love; "and the greatest of these is love." [18] Man is more than mind. So the scholar gets married and begets children. He atones for the mind's aloofness by cocktails in the faculty club and sometimes by worship in the church. Not even the abstractions of philosophy can escape the need for warmth and the longing for community, for the very word philosophy means the *love* of wisdom. Learning simply cannot survive in a loveless community. This little book would add: and human love cannot survive "the immitigable ferocity of self," [19] except it is held in the ultimate sanction of God's love. The word college loses its original meaning, for in many an instance it is no longer a group of colleagues older and younger intent on wisdom: it more resembles a series of atomized departments, each department being seamed by academic rivalries. Meanwhile the student secretly asks if the professor cares about him, for he may seem to care as little as Jove on Mount Olympus; and the lonely professor asks if the student cares about him, though academic aloofness allows him no such admission. How does love spread? By a shared devotion to some light and love above our human ways, not by any platform exhortations to brotherhood or by any whipped-up sentiment. If we trust that we are accepted of God's love, we can accept one another in that same love. We can accept even ourselves. Thus the Bible:

"In this is love, not that we loved God, but that he loved us, and sent his Son to be the expiation for our sins." [20] Outside the window against which these words are being written are two beds of zinnias: in one bed the plants are spindly, for it is in the shade of a tree; while the other, in benefit of the full sun, is a riot of color. Flowers of the mind also cannot flourish without a warmth from above and beyond their own life.

Why should German universities have sold out to Hitler or accepted him in silence? Perhaps they secretly despised him and his whole "brood of vipers," [21] but they made no effective protest. If they had spoken promptly and at risk, his threat might have been stayed and then annulled. Must we admit that their *Veritas*, defined as fact-finding or rationalism, had made only a vacuum into which he rushed, since human nature, not nature alone, abhors a vacuum? Perhaps every man in his essential manhood cries out for banners. Perhaps a mind greedy for facts leaves him as forlorn at last as a man greedy only for food. Perhaps cruel banners are better than no banners. Perhaps—the perhaps in this instance is bedrock surety—a man must worship in faith and hope and love. If he does not worship God, he still worships, for that is his manhood; but he then worships an idol, of sex or the state or some other twisted image, in perverted faith and hope and love. The mind is not separate. It is central in education, but there and always it is involved in man's total nature. St. Exupéry has moving passages [22] in which he tells us that love between a man and woman, or between colleagues in a collegium, does not come by their mutual admiration or even by their mutual loyalty, but as they look together to some mountain, its snows sunrise-tinted, challenging the illimitable sky. Then, he says, their hands search and clasp. Then love is found. Thus Biblical faith: "But we see Jesus." [23] He is better than a mountain. In Him are faith and hope and love.

These ponderings would seem to be confirmed as we confront the complexity of learning in any great university. At Harvard, which is "Fair Harvard" [24] by many a worthy test, the *Gazette* announces week by week a roster of lectures which is at once the joy and despair of any man who would learn. As for me, I am not only ignorant on many of the issues thus discussed; sometimes I can hardly pronounce the lecture titles. Learning is now so intricate and vast that a man who is well-versed in one discipline may be ignoramus in other disciplines. The resultant "confusion of tongues" is uneasy reminder of the Tower of Babel.[25] How is the confusion to be resolved? Not by "devotion to learning," for it is the learning which is divided, so divided that it turns scholars into strangers. Only a shared faith, a shared hope, and a shared love can now save our learning from locomotor ataxia, that is to say, from limbs that are heedless of any sovereign motive. There is positive instance at Harvard. At the Christmas Carol Service, which is thrice repeated because so many people wish to attend, all differences are transcended. The music is superlative in quality, but that fact is not the major magnet. Nor is it convincing to say, "For once theology is forgotten," for the carols themselves are outright theology. The reason is that "love came down at Christmas" [26]—the love disclosed in Jesus, the only love that can unify our dismembered learning and our chasmed earth. So the Bible world offers to education a profound faith and hope and love.

IV

These chapters are written in no defeatist mind. Secularism is not objectivity, but a faith after its own kind which is now being brought to challenge. A spate of books by both theologians and educators offers sufficient proof that the mind's adventure has struck tents in the secular land to seek a better country. Who knows where it may next pitch camp? There *are* verdicts to which men return and return. Signs appear that education may return to the Biblical faith which has long been its secret home. The Biblical faith in such a journey will not be Biblical faith as the Victorian era construed it, but Biblical faith as education itself has helped newly to interpret it—a faith illuminated by modern scholarship and rediscovered under the shocks and realities of our apocalyptic time. That faith, twisted by our finite hankerings, may easily become the "indoctrination" against which education rightly raises its barriers; but such indoctrination is now a smaller threat than an arid secularism. There is fear also that religious studies may become schismatic, but the tragedy of our age, with its massive idolatries and vaster bloodlettings, now sweeps us beyond that fear: "Modern Man is Obsolete" [27] unless our accepted modes are overcome by the breath of new life. There is a ground swell of student resolve to "know what religion is all about," and this also is evidence that old ways in education are now outmoded. Perhaps students dimly understand the truth of Arnold S. Nash's dictum that to give students more facts is like giving a drowning man more water.[28]

The prevailing patterns in education, as in the church, cannot quickly be changed. In the church our bourgeois culture has left a deep stain: the Protestant church is for the comfortable, and the comfortable wish it so, and even bring pressures on preachers that it may so continue; but the church is better than a bourgeois culture, for there is still confession of sins and still the astringent challenge of the Spirit. In education also there is a constant self-searching, as witness the repeated asking of the question, "What is education?" Perhaps the prevailing patterns should not suffer a violent change: revolutions are well named, for usually they only revolve. But change must come, for an arid rationalism plus a dreary factualism can no longer provide a home for the questing mind.

Matthew Arnold in his *Dover Beach* declared that "the Sea of Faith is at the ebb." He was right about his time, as we now realize, but not about our time. In our time, if we may hazard a guess that is not without evidence, the sea of faith is at the tremulous turn. He saw no bright future: only

> "a darkling plain
> Swept with confused alarm of struggle and flight,
> Where ignorant armies clash by night." [29]

Again he was tragically right. Then to what hope could he cling? To human love! "Ah, love, let us be true to one another." He was partly right: human love reflects a higher Love, but human love in itself is a weak reed;

for all things human are contingent and derived—they find sanction and sanctuary only in a higher Love. My own hope is that the household of faith and the realm of higher education may both return, each after its own order, to that Eternal constraint, and so serve one another and the common life.

Notes

Chapter 1

[1] William Shakespeare, *Love's Labour's Lost*, Act 1, sc. ii.

[2] *The Apostles' Creed.*

[3] Sigmund Freud, *Future of an Illusion*, trans. W. D. Robson-Scott (Garden City, New York: Doubleday Anchor Books, 1957), 83 f. See also Albert C. Outler, *Psychotherapy and the Christian Message* (New York: Harper and Bros., 1954), 199.

[4] Deut. 6:4; Mark 12:29.

[5] Psalm 24:1; I Cor. 10:26.

[6] Alfred North Whitehead, *Science and the Modern World* (New York: The Macmillan Co., 1926), ch. 1, particularly 18–19.

[7] Luke 6:48 R.S.V. See also Matt. 7:24–27.

[8] Title of a book by Henry Drummond, *The Ascent of Man* (London: Hodder and Stoughton, 1901), the Lowell Lectures.

[9] A town in Bavaria and the location of one of the notorious Nazi concentration camps.

[10] Gen. 2:7.

[11] Gen. 1:26, 27; 5:1.

[12] *General Education in a Free Society* (Cambridge: Harvard University Press, 1945), ch. 2, sec. i–ii, 40–41.

[13] William Shakespeare, *As You Like It*, Act 2, sc. vii.

[14] See D. R. G. Owen, *Body and Soul* (Philadelphia: The Westminster Press, 1956), 34–44, where he cites W. K. C. Guthrie, *Orpheus and Greek Religion* (London, Methuen and Co., Ltd., 1935).

[15] Martin Heidegger, *Existence and Being*, with an introduction by Werner Brock (Chicago: Henry Regnery Co., 1949), 84; John Wild, *The Challenge of Existentialism* (Bloomington: Indiana University Press, 1955), 75, 130 f., 175; David E. Roberts, *Existentialism and Religious Beliefs* (New York: Oxford University Press, 1957), 156, 166 f.; and John Macquarrie, *An Existentialist Theology* (New York: The Macmillan Co., 1955), 32, 59.

[16] Gen. 2:19–20.

[17] Martin Buber, *I and Thou*, trans. Ronald Gregor Smith (2nd ed.; New York: Charles Scribner's Sons, 1958), 52.

[18] Name of the farmer's wife (not seen but referred to jealously by Dame Ashfield) in Thomas Morton's play, *Speed the Plough* (1st ed. 1798; Philadelphia: Thomas R. Palmer, 1822).

[19] Phil. 1:23.

[20] William Shakespeare, *The Tempest,* Act 5, sc. i; also title of a book by Aldous Huxley, *Brave New World* (1st ed. 1932; New York: Harper and Bros., 1946). Huxley has used the title again in *Brave New World Revisited* (New York: Harper and Bros., 1958).

[21] Title of a book of sermons by David E. Robert, *The Grandeur and Misery of Man* (New York: Oxford University Press, 1955).

[22] Cantril Hadley, *The Invasion from Mars* (Princeton: Princeton University Press, 1952) contains a complete script of the Welles broadcast. See also Halford E. Luccock, *In the Minister's Workshop* (Nashville: Abingdon-Cokesbury Press, 1944), 156, for comments.

[23] Heb. 8:5.

[24] The Catechism: *The Book of Common Prayer* according to the use of the Protestant Episcopal Church.

[25] Gen. 2:5, 15.

[26] Luke 18:19 R.S.V.; Matt. 19:17.

[27] Sir Walter Moberly, *The Crisis in the University* (London: SCM Press Ltd., 1949).

[28] Zech. 9:13.

[29] John Maynard Keynes, *The End of the Laissez-Faire* (London: L. and V. Woolf, 1926).

[30] Karl Marx and Friedrich Engels, *The Communist Manifesto,* ed. Samuel H. Beer (New York: Appleton-Century-Crofts, Inc., 1955).

[31] German physicist, born 1901, won Nobel Prize for work on quantum theory. For an interesting discussion of his "Principle of Indeterminacy" see William G. Pollard, *Chance and Providence* (New York: Charles Scribner's Sons, 1958), 52 f., 138 f.

[32] Danish atomic physicist, born 1885, won Nobel Prize in 1922. Noted for his "Principle of Complementarity." See *ibid.,* 138, 141–52.

[33] Psalm 117:2.

[34] Psalm 145:13.

[35] Matt. 11:29.

[36] Psalm 90:1.

[37] See Paul Tillich, *Systematic Theology* (Chicago: University

of Chicago Press, 1951), I, 168–71, for an approach to this subject. See also Erich Fromm, *Man For Himself* (New York: Rinehart and Co., 1947), ch. 3, part 1, "The Human Situation"; and Carl Michalson, *Christianity and the Existentialists* (New York: Charles Scribner's Sons, 1956), 14–15.

Chapter 2

[1] René Descartes, *Discourse on the Method of Rightly Conducting the Reason and Seeking Truth in the Sciences* (Edinburgh: Sutherland and Knox, 1850), 75.

[2] Gen. 2:19–20.

[3] Gen. 1:26.

[4] Gen. 11:1–9.

[5] Alfred, Lord Tennyson, "Flower in the Crannied Wall," l. 5.

[6] William Wordsworth, "Expostulation and Reply," written in 1798, st. 7.

[7] Gen. 37:39–50.

[8] Sören Kierkegaard, *Concluding Unscientific Postscript*, trans. David F. Swenson and Walter Lowrie (Princeton: Princeton University Press, 1941), 275.

[9] See Oscar Cullman, *Christ and Time*, trans. Floyd V. Filson (Philadelphia: The Westminster Press, 1950), Part I, ch. 1; Paul Tillich, "Kairos," *A Handbook of Christian Theology* (New York: Living Age Books, 1958), 193; Erich Przywara, "Christian Root Terms in Religion and Culture," *Essays in Honor of Paul Tillich*, ed. Walter Leibrecht (New York: Harper and Bros., 1959), 113; and John A. T. Robinson, *In the End, God* (London: James Clarke and Co., Ltd.), ch. 4.

[10] From a prayer for the "Burial of the Dead," *Book of Common Order of the Church of Scotland* (London: Oxford University Press, 1957), 176.

[11] Wild, *The Challenge of Existentialism*, 54 f., 57–58, 160 f.

[12] Phil. 2:5; Luke 1:51.

[13] See Sören Kierkegaard, *The Concept of Dread*, trans. Walter Lowrie (Princeton: Princeton University Press, 1944); also references to "dread" in *The Journals of Sören Kierkegaard*, trans. Alexander Dru (New York: Oxford University Press, 1938);

Walter Lowrie, *Kierkegaard* (New York: Oxford University Press, 1938); and Wild, *The Challenge of Existentialism,* 35–37.

[14] Jean-Paul Sartre, *Being and Nothingness,* trans. Hazel E. Barnes (New York: Philosophical Library, 1956), particularly Part I, ch. 1, "The Problem of Nothingness"; David E. Roberts, *Existentialism and Religious Beliefs,* 195 f.; and Wild, *The Challenge of Existentialism,* 92–95, 161, 163–64, 166, 191–92.

[15] Archibald MacLeish, "The End of the World," *Collected Poems 1927–1952* (Boston: Houghton Mifflin and Co., 1952), 23.

[16] Gen. 1:26, 27; 5:1.

[17] Acts 17:28.

[18] Heidegger, *Existence and Being,* 51, 55–57, 61–64, 67, 74 f.; Roberts, *Existentialism and Religious Beliefs,* 151 ff.; and Wild, *The Challenge of Existentialism,* 41, 47, 50, 69, 115, 126–29.

[19] Sigmund Freud, *The Ego and the Id,* trans. Joan Riviere (London: Hogarth Press, 1950).

[20] William Shakespeare, *Hamlet, Prince of Denmark.*

[21] *Ibid.,* Act 3, sc. i.

[22] Zech. 9:13.

[23] John Dewey, *Psychology* (New York: Harper and Bros., 1889), ch. xviii, "Development of Volition," particularly 370.

[24] *The Book of Common Prayer,* second Collect.

[25] Adolf Hitler, *Mein Kampf,* chapters on "People and Race" and "The State," and *My Struggle* (London: Hurst and Blackett, Ltd., 1933), Part I, ch. xi; and William L. Shirer, *Berlin Diary* (New York: Alfred Knopf, 1941), 582.

[26] Rom. 1:21.

[27] John Milton, *Paradise Lost,* Book 2, l. 113—actually a saying of Aristotle. See E. M. Cope, *An Introduction to Aristotle's Rhetoric* (London: The Macmillan Co., 1867), 267 citing *Rhetorica,* Book 2, ch. 24.

[28] Tillich, *Systematic Theology,* Part I, ch. ii, particularly 108–18.

[29] Hitler, *supra* note 25, ch. 2.

[30] Francis Thompson, "The Hound of Heaven," *The Works of Francis Thompson: Poems* (2 vols., London: Burns, Oates and Washbourne, Ltd., 1925), I, 111.

[31] Exod. 3.

[32] Edna St. Vincent Millay, "God's World," *Poems* (London: Martin Secker, 1923), 22.

[33] See for example Isa. 10–12; Mic. 1.

[34] Archibald MacLeish, *Panic* (Boston: Houghton Mifflin Co., 1935), 18.

[35] Paul Sabatier, *Life of St. Francis of Assisi* (New York: Charles Scribner's Sons, 1927), 289–90.

[36] Psalm 115:3.

[37] Dr. Ralph F. Miller and Dr. Robert W. Quinn of the Medical School of Dartmouth College (Mary Hitchcock Hospital), lost on Feb. 21, 1959; their plane and messages found on May 7, 1959. See the *Boston Daily Globe,* May 7 and May 8, 1959, and the *New York Times* of the same dates.

[38] Tillich, *supra* note 9, ch. 2.

[39] See C. H. Dodd, *The Interpretation of the Fourth Gospel* (Cambridge: Harvard University Press, 1955), 170 f.; R. H. Strachan, *The Fourth Gospel* (London: SCM Press, 1941), 141 f.; Alan Richardson, *An Introduction to the Theology of the New Testament* (New York: Harper and Bros., 1958), 112; and Albert C. Outler, "Quid est Veritas?" *The Christian Century* (March 4, 1959).

[40] John Drinkwater, *Abraham Lincoln* (Boston: Houghton Mifflin Co., 1919), sc. iii, 72.

Chapter 3

[1] See an article by Samuel Eliot Morison, "Harvard Seals and Arms," *The Harvard Graduates' Magazine* (September, 1933). In summary: the *Veritas* shield design, discovered in the Archives by President Quincy, was displayed by him at the Bicentennial, 1836, and voted the common seal of the college in 1843. The seal bearing *Christo et Ecclesiae,* probably introduced by the Puritan Divine, William Ames, replaced an earlier (1650) seal, *In Christo Gloria,* and was in use as early as 1693. It was voted official by the Corporation in 1847. After a tempest over the seals, created by Oliver Wendell Holmes's two odes in 1878, a new vote became necessary and the present "Appleton Seal" (*Christo et Ecclesiae* surrounding the *Veritas* shield) was adopted in 1885 as the official "great seal" of the University. Since about 1910 the *Veritas* shield (used by the library since 1846), without the surrounding inscription, has become, by common usage, the insignia used by buildings, departments, etc.

[2] John 1:14 R.S.V.

[3] Leslie H. Allen, *Bryan and Darrow at Dayton* (New York: Arthur Lee and Co., 1925) contains a full account of the Scopes Trial.

[4] Matt. 22:37; Mark 12:30; Luke 10:27.

[5] *New York Times,* August 18, 1959.

[6] Huxley, *Brave New World.*

[7] John Masefield, "Biography," *Poems and Plays* (New York: The Macmillan Co., 1921).

[8] Acts 17:28.

[9] I recall reading this phrase in a newspaper account of an educators' conference.

[10] II Cor. 5:7.

[11] Charles Mills Gayley, *The Classic Myths* (Chicago: Ginn and Co., 1911).

[12] *The Satires of Decimus Junius Juvenalis,* trans. William Gifford (London: W. Bulmer and Co., 1806), Satire vii, v. 71, 232.

[13] I Cor. 13:12.

[14] Ralph Waldo Emerson, "Ode," inscribed to W. H. Channing, st. 7.

[15] Rev. 13:8.

[16] Corliss Lamont, *A Humanist Funeral Service* (Boston: Beacon Press, 1947).

[17] Sartre, *Being and Nothingness.*

[18] I Cor. 13:13 R.S.V.

[19] Robert Penn Warren, *Brother to Dragons, A Tale in Verse and Voices* (New York: Random House, 1953), words given to Thomas Jefferson.

[20] 1 John 4:10 R.S.V.

[21] Matt. 3:7 R.S.V.

[22] Antoine de Saint Exupéry, *Wind, Sand and Stars, Airman's Odyssey* (New York: Harcourt, Brace and Co., 1940), 27–28, 195.

[23] Heb. 2:9.

[24] Title of the Harvard Ode, composed by the Reverend Samuel Gilman who graduated from Harvard in 1811 and for forty years was pastor of the Unitarian Church in Charleston, S.C. The Ode was sung for the first time at the Bicentennial, 1836. These words are also used as title of a book descriptive of Harvard by Samuel Chamberlain, with a text by Donald Moffat (New York: Hastings House, 1948).

[25] Gen. 11:1–9.

26 "Christmastide," *The Poetical Works of Christina Georgina Rossetti* (London: The Macmillan Co., 1924), 159, st. 1.

27 Norman Cousins, *Modern Man Is Obsolete* (New York: Viking Press, 1945).

28 Arnold S. Nash, *The University and the Modern World* (New York: The Macmillan Co., 1944), 139.

29 Matthew Arnold, *Poems* (New York: E. P. Dutton and Co., Inc., 1948), 85–86.

Index